LEAD ANYWAY

FLYING ABOVE LIFE'S CHAOS AND TURBULENCE

ROBERT ANDERSON, JR.

FREILING
AGENCY

Published by Freiling Agency, LLC.

P.O. Box 1264
Warrenton, VA 20188

www.FreilingAgency.com

HB ISBN: 978-1-963701-66-1
E-book ISBN: 978-1-963701-67-8

CONTENTS

Introduction: Lead Anyway............................v

1   Clear Your Mind...............................1

2   Learning to Lead, Alone...................11

3   Leading When You Can't Fix It.......19

4   Push, Not Pull 27

5   Leading Through the Pain................35

6   You Don't Know What You Don't
Know 43

7   You're Not Always the Person You
Thought You Were...........................51

8   Lead Through the Noise...................57

9   Lead With Purpose 65

10   Boundaries Bite................................73

11   We Live On 81

12   Best Man..89

Conclusion: Lead Anyway...........................99

"The only person you are destined to become is the person you decide to be."

—Ralph Waldo Emerson

INTRODUCTION

LEAD ANYWAY

Let's start with a bit of context—this is my third book.

In my first book, *L.E.T.S. Lead*, I explored the foundations of leadership: how to step forward, take initiative, and guide others with greater clarity and purpose. In *Scaling Smart*, I focused on business—specifically, the leadership traits necessary for growing and scaling an organization without losing your integrity in the process. Both books, like this one, draw deeply from my journey.

As a national security expert and seasoned executive, I've had the privilege of serving on both private and publicly traded company boards. My focus has always been on aligning risk and security with broader business strategy—helping Fortune 500 companies navigate crises, develop strategic plans, and mitigate long-term threats. I bring a mindset forged in the field—first as a Delaware state trooper, then as a senior FBI executive and member of the elite Hostage Rescue Team. I've led major criminal investigations and national security operations in cybersecurity, counterintelligence, intellectual property theft, and critical incident response.

My leadership philosophy is grounded in real-world experience—marked by pragmatism, focus, and a relentless drive for results. Whether in the boardroom or in the middle of a national emergency, I've had to learn— sometimes the hard way—how to turn chaos into strategy and risk into opportunity. I don't claim to be a leadership guru. But I've been in the trenches. And I've learned, over time, that leadership is less about charisma and more about consistency—less about being in charge—and more about showing up.

This book—*Lead Anyway*—is the natural next step in that journey. It's about motivation, resilience, and the mindset required to rise above life's daily chaos. Because leadership, at its core, isn't about position or power. It's about showing up—especially when things get hard. And it always gets hard.

Suppose you've ever led anything—a team, a company, a project, or even a family—you already know that leadership rarely unfolds in a straight line. It gets messy. It gets frustrating. And sometimes, it just feels like too much. I've been there. This book is about the moments that make you want to quit but demand that you lead anyway.

One of my greatest influences has always been Dr. Norman Vincent Peale. His message of positive thinking shaped much of my approach to both leadership and life. He once said:

"Change your thoughts, and you change your world."

That's more than a motivational quote. It's a leadership imperative. In times of chaos, your mindset becomes either your greatest asset or your biggest liability. Leaders don't always get to choose their circumstances. But they do get to choose their response. I didn't learn that lesson overnight. Nobody does.

So this book brings together the themes of my previous work through the lens of motivation and mental resilience in the face of chaos. You'll find real stories here—from business, yes, but also from personal experiences. Some are victories. Some are hard lessons. All of them offer insight into what it takes to lead when life doesn't go according to plan.

This is a book about leadership, but it's also a book about life. It's about showing up with courage. It's about keeping your footing when everything around you is shaking. And ultimately, it's about triumphing over chaos. Not by avoiding it, but by learning how to lead anyway.

We All Need a Little Help Sometimes

Let's be honest: we all need help with leadership and motivation. In today's fast-paced, high-pressure world, it's not just our jobs that demand more of us. It's our personal lives, our families, our businesses, our class-rooms. The demands keep piling up, and the stress can hit hard. Sometimes, it shows up suddenly and knocks you off your feet. Other times, it creeps in quietly and slowly drains your energy and confidence.

Everyone faces struggles. Everyone deals with frustration. I'm no different. And I want to speak out loud about the stuff most of us deal with in silence—the doubts, the setbacks, the pressure that chips away at our motivation. We all carry chaos. We all have pain points.

For some, it's procrastination. For others, it's goal-setting, fear of failure, or that gnawing sense of inadequacy. Whatever the root, the result is often the same: we feel stuck, discouraged, or unsure of what to do next. And most of us don't give ourselves enough credit. We're too busy being our own harshest critic. If you're anything like me, you know what that feels like—analyzing everything, second-guessing yourself, holding yourself to impossible standards. And from the outside? No one sees it. But on the inside, it's exhausting!

That's why I wrote this book. It's not a leadership manual. It's a real-world conversation about moving forward in the middle of chaos, stress, and self-doubt. It's a collection of honest stories—sometimes messy, always meaningful. Because that's where motivation lives—in the quiet victories and the daily choices that keep us going.

We all want to be better. We all want more joy, peace, and meaning. I believe we can get there by facing it head-on. You're not alone. And if these stories help you feel seen, inspired, or just a little less discouraged, then this book has done its job.

Learning to Lead Through the Chaos

In *L.E.T.S. Lead*, I introduced the idea of "Leadership Moments"—those specific points in time when you're faced with a challenge, a decision, or an opportunity to lead. This book takes that concept further. It's a deeper dive into the real moments that tested me—not just as a leader but as a person.

The stories in this book span decades. Some are small moments with significant meaning. Others were defining experiences that shifted my worldview. They're not polished case studies. They're real. Each one taught me how to treat people better, lead stronger, and stay grounded—even when everything around me wasn't.

What do I mean by "chaos"?

To me, chaos is a state of confusion and disorder. It's when life feels unmanageable and out of control. And for someone who values order and structure, chaos presses all the wrong buttons. It disrupts. It distracts. And most of all, it makes you feel powerless.

But here's the truth: chaos isn't always the enemy. It's a teacher. It reveals character. It forces decisions. And if we let it, it can sharpen us. That's what this book explores. Not just how to stay motivated but how to lead when things get hard. When the pressure is on, when the plan falls apart, when you're out of options and unsure of the next step, those are the moments that define you.

Everyday Chaos: The Stuff We All Deal With

Chaos doesn't always arrive like a hurricane. Most of the time, it sneaks in quietly—through stress, interruptions, and small things that build up over time. Here are a few forms of everyday chaos you'll recognize:

- **Lack of Order:** A messy desk. A cluttered garage. A calendar is full of overlapping obligations. When routines break down, stress ramps up.

- **Unpredictability:** Life doesn't care about your schedule. The car won't start. A kid forgets their backpack. The Wi-Fi crashes before a Zoom call. All of it tests your flexibility.

- **Overwhelm:** Too many tasks. Too little time. Ten small things that pile up and make your head spin.

- **Confusion:** Poor communication. Conflicting expectations. Shifting priorities. It creates frustration—even when the goals are clear.

- **The Morning Rush:** If you've got kids, you get it. Mornings are a contact sport.

- **A Busy Workday:** You start with a plan. Then come the calls, the questions, the fires to put out. Before you know it, your whole day's derailed.

- **Household Mayhem:** Dishes, laundry, sick pets, spilled juice—real life rarely pauses for you to catch up.

This isn't just noise. It's the backdrop of the modern life we all live in.

Let's zoom out for a second.

Globally, we're dealing with geopolitical tension, economic instability, and the erosion of public trust. Conflict abroad and division at home affect everything from gas prices to grocery bills. Technology is racing ahead, but so is misinformation. Our politics are polarized. Our attention is fractured. And our collective anxiety is rising.

People feel stuck. They feel overwhelmed. And they're not wrong to feel that way. When you stack global stress on top of personal stress, leadership becomes more than a professional skill—it becomes a survival skill.

This book isn't a method. It's not a formula. It's a collection of true stories—some from my youth, some from recent trials—that show what it means to lead through the mess. Because most people aren't fighting wars or running Fortune 500s, they're fighting the daily grind. The pressure. The weight of responsibility. The fear of not measuring up.

And that's where authentic leadership begins. You can rise above the chaos. You can lead through it. You can *lead anyway.*

"It always seems
impossible until it's done."
—Nelson Mandela

1

CLEAR YOUR MIND

In today's high-stress world, mental clarity might be the most underrated leadership skill. You can have all the technical knowledge, experience, and confidence in the world—but when life throws you into a high-speed crisis, none of it matters if your mind isn't calm. In those moments, your ability to clear your head and focus is the difference between disaster and survival—between reacting and leading.

This story begins with my friend, Jimmy. Jimmy was stuck to the ceiling!

This was many years ago, in another life, when I was in the government. Two friends and I were in Salt Lake City, preparing to fly a brand-new Bell 412 helicopter back to Virginia. It was winter, and we wanted to take off early to beat the winds that tore across the mountains once the sun came up.

The Bell 412 is no toy. It's a versatile, twin-engine utility helicopter—renowned for reliability and adaptability across all types of missions. Its design allows it to operate in extreme environments. But flying over Utah's Wasatch Range in winter isn't something you take lightly. With peaks reaching up to nearly 12,000 feet—like Mount Nebo and Timpanogos—you're flirting with an environment that doesn't forgive mistakes.

To put it in perspective, the FAA requires pilots to use supplemental oxygen above 12,500 feet MSL for more than 30 minutes, and above 14,000 feet, it's needed full-time. At 15,000 feet, even passengers are required to be on oxygen.

And it's not just altitude. Flying on the leeward side of mountains in winter can generate violent turbulence and sudden downdrafts—currents of air that can suck an aircraft toward the ground and leave even experienced pilots scrambling to maintain control.

That morning, though, it was beautiful. Cold. Clear. No wind. Moonlight shimmering off snow-covered ridges. We had coffee in hand and purpose in our stride as we walked out to the helicopter.

I was flying first, so I climbed into the left front seat. My copilot took the right. Jimmy, a longtime friend and fellow pilot, was riding in the back, perched on top of an empty cooler—because all the rear seats had been removed for reupholstering. Typically, the 412 accommodates up to 14 passengers in the rear. It's a big bird.

We ran through the checklist.

Engine 1 Start. Fuel Transfer switch ON.

Engine 1 Fuel Transfer caution light extinguished.

Engine 1 Boost Pump switch ON.

Boost Pump light extinguished. Fuel pressure is OK.

Rotor clear.

Start switch—Engine 1.

ITT rising… wait… wait… abort!

The engine rolled offline—a false start.

We all exchanged looks. "That's not right," I said. They agreed.

We tried again—same outcome. The engine failed to stabilize.

We shut it down and headed back into the FBO to call maintenance. Several hours and a dozen phone calls later, we had answers. Nothing major. It's just enough of a problem to cost us our window of calm weather.

The wind had picked up. The clouds were starting to move. The sun was climbing higher, and we still had 13 to 18 hours of flying ahead of us—depending on the wind.

Finally, both engines lit up smoothly. Everything checked out. I took us airborne.

Climbing over the mountains, we started the trip toward Virginia.

At first, the air was smooth. The mountains looked like something out of a painting—majestic, serene. But looks can be deceiving.

The turbulence hit fast.

Suddenly, the helicopter lurched violently. We were in a downdraft. The air that had supported us was now yanking us downward like a steel trap.

The Vertical Speed Indicator pinned at 6,000 feet per minute—down at full power.

I was slammed up into my five-point harness. Papers and manuals tore free and swirled. The rotor wash turned to a scream. Caution lights lit up like a Christmas tree. Every emergency warning you don't want to see was happening—all at once.

Instinctively, I glanced back to check on Jimmy.

He was gone.

I looked again. No cooler. No Jimmy. Just a big, terrifying void in the back of the aircraft.

The doors were shut. Nothing was broken—no sign of a breach.

"Clear your mind."

That was the voice in my head. Not panic. Not fear. Just focus. I forced myself to slow down my breathing and turned again—deliberate this time.

And that's when I looked up.

There he was.

Jimmy was stuck to the ceiling. The cooler, too. All the loose papers were floating beside them, pinned by the negative Gs. Jimmy's eyes were the size of silver dollars.

All I could manage was: "Hang in there!"

He didn't answer. He didn't have to. His face said everything.

We fought the controls—collective up, cyclic steady. The machine bucked and shuddered. My co-pilot and I worked as one. Every movement was deliberate. We had trained for this, but training doesn't make it easy.

Finally, we hit a sliver of rising air.

The rotors bit in. The VSI stopped falling. We clawed back altitude.

And that's when Jimmy came crashing down.

Along with the cooler, the paperwork, and everything else that had defied gravity moments before. It was loud. Way louder than I expected. Jimmy gasped for air and strapped in—without needing to be told.

No one said a word. Not then. Not for the rest of the flight over those mountains.

We pressed on, grateful for altitude. Thankful to be alive.

Landing on solid ground never felt so good.

Leadership Moment: The Power of Mental Clarity in Crisis

What saved us that day wasn't just skill. It wasn't just training. It was the ability to stay focused when every instinct in my body was telling me to panic. In leadership—and life—crises will come. Downdrafts you never saw coming—chaos you didn't cause. And people depend on you for guidance in the middle of it.

When that happens, you can't afford to lose your mind. You have to clear it. You have to focus.

For me, it meant seeing what was right in front of me—but looking again. Slowing down when everything inside screamed to rush. That single act—clearing my mind—let me spot Jimmy and refocus on what mattered most. But you don't need to be in a helicopter to learn this. You might be facing a volatile market, a team in disarray, a business problem you can't fix, or a family crisis that keeps you up at night.

The same principles apply:

- Breathe.

- Focus on the controllable.

- Fly the aircraft first—meaning: handle the most critical need first.

- Re-establish perspective.

- And when necessary, look again.

Leadership isn't about having all the answers. It's about remaining calm enough to find the next right one—even when everything's upside down. And that starts when you clear your mind.

"The only limit to our
realization of tomorrow will be
our doubts of today."
—Franklin D. Roosevelt

2

LEARNING TO LEAD, ALONE

Boardrooms or business books don't always shape leadership. Sometimes, the earliest and most profound lessons come from moments we never saw coming. This chapter explores trauma, resilience, and the long road to recovery. Because leadership is forged not just in how we lead others, but in how we recover, rebuild, and move forward from pain. That's what I learned at age nine when a Cadillac taught me that life comes fast. Sometimes hits harder than you can imagine.

In 1974, the epitome of cool to me was a bright blue Schwinn Varsity bicycle. It was a ten-speed, sleek time machine that would propel me from my little ranch house in my development in Wilmington, Delaware, to my friend Fran's house two miles away in just minutes.

The fading summer sunlight cast long shadows as I pedaled homeward from Fran's house. I was maybe nine or ten at most, and the world stretched out before me, a canvas of endless possibilities. The familiar rhythm of the wheels against the asphalt was a comforting soundtrack to my youthful reverie. The air was thick with the scent of freshly cut grass and the lingering warmth of the day.

My development was a maze of winding roads and identical ranch-style houses, with some two-story split-levels thrown in, much like the Brady Bunch house on TV. I knew every curve, every dip, every patch of cracked pavement. I approached the familiar corner where a towering pine tree stood, its thick trunk obscuring the view of oncoming traffic. I leaned into the turn. The Schwinn responded with practiced ease.

Suddenly, a dark shape loomed into view. An older model Cadillac. A hulking behemoth of a car. Its chrome glinting menacingly.

There was no time to react. The collision was instantaneous. I hit it head-on. No braking. No swerving. Just impact.

I was airborne. Propelled forward with terrifying force. The world spun a dizzying kaleidoscope of asphalt and sky. My hands still gripped the handlebars. My body wasn't ready. My face hit the pavement with full momentum.

Pain. Blinding, searing pain. My mouth filled with blood. My front tooth tore through my lip and broke clean off. To this day, when I smile, you can see where they fixed it. A reminder every single day.

Through the haze, I saw the wreckage of my beloved Schwinn. The front wheel was mangled, grotesquely embedded in the Cadillac's shattered windshield. The driver, a middle-aged man, scrambled out. His face a blur of concern—and then, something colder. He was staring at the car. Not me. Assessing the damage.

Then he turned and told me, "Just walk it off." No apology. No offer to help. It's just a dismissive wave. He told me to walk the mangled bike home. Shocked, bleeding, and in pain. That's what I did.

I gripped the twisted handlebars. The walk, usually a ten-minute ride, became a long, painful odyssey. With each step, the weight of the Schwinn, its front wheel still jammed in the Cadillac's windshield mocked me. The Cadillac followed behind, my broken tire still lodged in its front glass.

By the time I reached my house, I could barely see straight. No one answered when I called out. I made my way to the one room in the house with air conditioning. It's where my Dad cooled off before work on summer days. He was asleep.

"Dad, I got hit by a car." Nothing. "Dad!"

One eye opened. Then both. He shot up. Alarm on his face. Then, there was a crash outside. We ran out to see the Cadillac speeding off. The driver had finally yanked the tire from his windshield and dumped it in the street like trash.

The hours that followed were full of sirens, x-rays, stitches, and silence. The doctors pieced my lips together. They examined my head. They took x-rays of my mouth. My parents were shaken. I saw it in their eyes: the unspoken question—*What if?* The Schwinn never rode again. It sat in the garage, a mangled monument until it was hauled away. I avoided that corner for years. The towering pine tree, once just a landmark, became a trigger.

But that day changed me. The pain was one thing. But the injustice? That left a deeper scar. I learned how fast life changes. I knew that some people walk away from their damage. And I realized that healing is personal—it doesn't come all at once, and it rarely comes easy.

Leadership Moment: When Life Hits You Hard

Triumphing over chaos in both your personal and business life is linked to leadership and motivation. And this story—painful as it was—showed me why. It's about learning to look ahead and lead through confusion, injury, and adversity. It's about the slow walk back from pain—physical and emotional— and how that process builds grit, awareness, and empathy.

Here's how it applies:

The Nature of Chaos: Chaos isn't just found in emergencies or crises. Sometimes, it's a personal moment of pain or injustice that shakes us. Chaos can manifest as an accident, an unexpected diagnosis, or even just the wrong person showing up at the worst possible time. It can shut us down—or call us up.

Leadership in the Face of Chaos begins with clarity. Even as a kid, I knew what I had to do: get home. A leader sets the destination first. Similarly, leaders must identify what matters most at the moment. That focus brings strength. The pain I felt on that long walk wasn't just physical—it was emotional. But every step forward was a quiet act of courage. Strength builds through motion.

Then comes the moment to act. Sometimes, leadership means carrying the weight alone. You might be the only one who believes it's possible. Do it anyway. No one was coming to rescue me, and no one may be coming to rescue you. Take action anyway. Authentic leadership often happens when no one's watching. People don't need perfect leaders. They need present ones. If you've lived through pain and kept moving, you're more qualified to lead than you think.

Here's one more thing: leaders don't always get to pick the moment they're called to rise. Sometimes, it shows up at the corner of your neighborhood on a bike ride home. Sometimes, it's not a business decision—it's a decision to stand back up, face the pain, and move forward. If you've ever been blind-sided by life and kept going, you're already a leader. Now, imagine who else you might help do the same.

"Success is not final, failure is

not fatal: it is the courage to

continue that counts."

—Winston Churchill

3

LEADING WHEN YOU CAN'T FIX IT

Some leadership lessons don't come with manuals. They crash into your life in the middle of the night. They jolt you awake—not just physically, but spiritually. This chapter is about what happens when the person you thought was invincible is suddenly human. When you're a kid watching your father fight for his life on a green sofa soaked in summer sweat. When leadership, for the first time, becomes real—not about commanding others, but about holding steady when the world around you unravels.

I was about 14. It was summer in Wilmington, Delaware, and even at 2 a.m., the air was thick, hot, and still. I woke up to the sound of my mother and aunt making noise in the living room. Our house—a tiny three-bedroom ranch with shag green carpet and orange kitchen walls—wasn't anything special. We had one and a half bathrooms. No air conditioning. And no money.

We were probably the poorest family in our middle-class neighborhood. The house was the worst on the block, not because we didn't care, but because my dad's business was up and down. Sporadic income, nonstop work. He did what he could. We all did.

I walked out of my bedroom and headed down the narrow hallway toward the living room. The front door was wide open, and the screen door latched. The only relief from the 90-degree heat. Back then, Dad was proud that we lived in a neighborhood where you could leave your front door open.

But nothing felt safe that night.

I turned the corner—and everything stopped.

My mother and aunt were hunched over my father, trying to hold him upright on the green sofa with its maroon pillows. My father was a big man, a World War II vet, my hero. He looked broken. His face was green. His right hand clutched his chest. His left arm dangled at his side. His eyes were full of pain and fear. My mom was crying. My aunt was yelling into the kitchen phone; its long, curly cord stretched into chaos. She couldn't get 911 to work. She was panicking.

And I froze.

I had never seen my father like that. He was the strongest man I knew. And in an instant, he was mortal. Collapsing into the cushions that suddenly seemed too soft to support him.

My world narrowed to the shape of that room.

It was a strange kind of chaos, the kind where time stretches and contracts. Where you want to move, but your feet won't. Where you feel small and powerless and full of fear so cold it burns.

The sounds blurred. The room spun. I remember wondering if I could do CPR. My hands were shaking. I was barely breathing.

I was watching the only man I'd ever looked up to fight for every breath. And then— sirens. The wail of approaching paramedics cut through the heat and the panic. It was the most comforting sound I had ever heard. It brought order. Focus. Hope.

The EMTs arrived quickly and calmly. They took over. Their voices were steady. Their actions exact. It was the first time I saw what real leadership looked like under pressure. The hospital became our second home. A world of beeping machines, fluorescent lights, and tense silence. The ICU felt like another planet. My dad was covered in tubes. I barely recognized him. The man who used to toss me a baseball now couldn't lift his hand.

We didn't know if he'd survive. Every hour was a question mark. I stopped sleeping. I stopped eating. I stopped thinking about myself altogether. That was new for me, thinking about someone else.

My mom was falling apart. So I tried to stay strong. I stopped playing baseball to help with Dad's business. I loved baseball. I never played again as a kid. We didn't have money for emergencies. I never noticed that until then. Everything felt fragile—our income, our family, our future. And me? I couldn't even drive.

That summer changed me. I saw how fast things fall apart. I saw what love looks like under pressure. I saw how chaos isn't just something that happens outside. It explodes inside you, too. But I also learned something else: you don't stay frozen forever. Eventually, my dad pulled through. It was a long road. Recovery was slow and laborious. But we found strength. We endured. And I started to see life differently. I began to understand just how short and precious it is.

Leadership Moment: When Strength Fails, Clarity Leads

There's a moment in every leader's life when someone they look up to becomes vulnerable. That moment either breaks you or shapes you. For me, it did both. I learned that leadership isn't about power—it's about presence. It's about standing still when everything in you wants to run. It's about showing up in the chaos, even when you don't have the answers.

In those days, I couldn't solve anything. I couldn't fix his heart. I couldn't stop the fear. But I could stay. I could be there. I could take on responsibility. And in that, I became something new: dependable. That summer taught me the art of quiet leadership—leading by caring, by listening, by taking small but necessary steps. It also taught me how chaos breaks the illusion of control. It humbles you. It reminds you of how little you have figured out. But it is in that humility that wisdom begins.

Looking back now, I realize it's no coincidence I became a Delaware State Trooper and eventually a Trooper Paramedic. That night planted a seed. I never named it, but it grew anyway. Because you never know how you grow until you look back and connect the pain to your purpose.

There's a reason why we pause when we reflect on our parents' mortality. It hits

differently. It forces us to ask hard questions. What really matters? Who do I need
to become? What's worth holding onto?
That summer was a crash course in mortality,
maturity, and meaning. It showed me the
weight of love. It introduced me to suffering.
And it built a foundation I didn't even know
I'd need. So if you're in a season of chaos—if
someone you love is hurting, if your world
feels like it's collapsing—don't dismiss it.
You're being shaped. You're becoming. And
someday, you'll look back and say: *That's
when I started to lead.*

"A good plan violently
executed now is better than
a perfect plan executed
next week."
—General George S. Patton

4

PUSH, NOT PULL

There's a lesson I learned late in life that I wish I had learned earlier: leaders don't wait. They don't wait to be asked how someone's doing. They don't wait for information to be requested. They push. In relationships, in business, in family, in life. Proactively sharing information with friends and family, rather than waiting for them to request it, fosters stronger connections and demonstrates genuine care. That's true leadership.

When I was at the FBI, this concept was not just a helpful idea—it was the difference between life and death. My job often required me to take chaotic, incomplete, even frightening information—and push it up the chain before anyone asked for it. You don't wait until the danger knocks. You send a warning. You stay ahead of the threat. If I waited for someone to pull the information from me, we'd lose valuable time. Time that could cost lives. Whether we were tracking organized crime, identifying terrorist threats, or monitoring national security vulnerabilities, my role was to identify patterns, anticipate potential dangers, and communicate them early. Loudly. Clearly. Proactively. Pushing that information meant protecting lives. That mindset became a defining leadership trait.

But it's not just an FBI thing. This idea applies everywhere.

In our increasingly busy lives, time and attention are in short supply. But a short "thinking of you" message, an article someone would appreciate, or a reminder they didn't know they needed. Those are signals that someone is watching out for you. And those moments matter. I've learned that when we push information, we're not just passing along data. We're showing we care.

This works in all aspects of our lives. At home, in business, and friendships. Pushing information creates opportunities for meaningful, personalized connections. Sharing a recipe you know someone will love or a resource they might need—that's more than just communication. That's leading. That's motivating. That's caring with purpose.

In contrast, waiting for others to pull information (which is reactive) limits connection. It leaves people feeling alone. It's better to control the outcome by being proactive. When you push, you guide. When you wait to be asked, you react. And reactive leadership always lags.

We live in a world that's spread out and always on the move. Family members across states or continents. Friends we rarely see. But when we push photos, stories, videos, or even short texts, we bridge that distance. We close the gap. We create presence. But here's the thing: if you're like me, you might be private. You might not love reaching out first. It's hard. But it's worth it. That push builds trust, strengthens connections, and leads to growth. Yes, when you take a risk, you open yourself up to rejection or ridicule. Not everyone wants to engage. But you'll never grow deeper relationships by staying quiet. Leaders initiate. Leaders risk. Leaders lean in.

I've spent my life studying people—how they think, how they work, how they communicate. Whether I'm in a boardroom, a briefing, or on stage giving a keynote, I know this to be true: pulling information limits insight. Pushing creates possibility. Pushing information also empowers. It helps others navigate the chaos. Sharing an article during a stressful time or giving someone a heads-up before things go sideways. That's what leadership looks like. That's real support, especially when others are too overwhelmed to ask for help.

So here's a different way to think about it:

The Push of Ambition vs. the Pull of Comfort: We all want to grow, but it's easier to stay comfortable. Growth demands push. Pushing out of comfort means risking failure, discomfort, or the unknown—but it's also the only path to transformation. Ambition doesn't wait to be invited. It knocks the door down.

The Push for Independence vs. the Pull of Belonging: We want autonomy. We also wish to connect. Pushing into one shouldn't mean abandoning the other. Great leaders learn how to stand on their own and still reach out to others. The real strength lies in knowing when to do both.

The Push of Innovation vs. the Pull of Tradition: Leaders push boundaries while still honoring what works. Innovation requires challenging the norm, stepping into discomfort, and asking "What if?" without losing sight of the values and practices that built your foundation. The best leaders innovate with respect.

The Push of Fear vs. the Pull of Courage: Courage is not the absence of fear. It's pushing through despite it. It's showing up in the complicated conversation. It's stepping forward in the face of uncertainty. Every great leader has felt fear—but they acted anyway.

The Push of Logic vs. the Pull of Emotion: Sometimes logic leads. Sometimes empathy does. Authentic leadership respects both. You can't data your way through every human moment. Sometimes, the right call is the one that feels right, not just the one that adds up on paper.

You get the idea. The point is this: in every area of life, pushing takes intention, strength, and care. Whether it's a message to a friend, a warning up the chain of command, or a word of encouragement to your child, leadership starts with the decision to speak first, not wait to be asked.

And the best leaders—the ones we remember, the ones we trust—didn't just pull us along. They pushed us forward.

"Our greatest glory is not in never falling, but in rising every time we fall."

—Ralph Waldo Emerson

5

LEADING THROUGH
THE PAIN

Y ou are going to love this story.
Unfortunately, it's true—like everything
I write about!

At six years old, the world was a vast playground. My days were filled with trips to
my father's horse business, baseball, scraped
knees, grass-stained clothes, and the bound-
less energy of childhood. One sunny afternoon that carefree existence was abruptly
shattered.

It was spring, a perfect day—no clouds, a
light breeze, not hot, not cold. I was playing
outside and decided to wander down my
neighborhood to explore. Back then, your
parents didn't always know where you were.

They'd just say, "Be home by supper time!" No cell phones. No social media. Just freedom— and, looking back, a fair bit of danger.

I wandered down the street and saw Mike and Mac working on the roof of Mike's house. Mike was a postman, and Mac was his neighbor and a carpenter. Both were in their fifties and good friends of my parents. They had been replacing Mike's roof and gutters, and the front yard was full of debris and all kinds of things that a young boy found fascinating.

Mike and Mac said hi and explicitly told me to be careful and not walk around the front yard. Naturally, I didn't listen. While they got back to work, I began exploring from the side yard. First, I inspected the old shingles and plywood, then started building a small castle from the broken materials. I was having a great time—feeling invincible.

Then I saw it. The holy grail: a long, 20-foot piece of gutter lying upside down among the debris. It had the longest nails I had ever seen—at least 12 inches, painted white to match the gutter. It looked just like a balance beam. My sister had done gymnastics, and this seemed like something I could do even better.

I'd walked the "balance beam" a few times when I saw a long nail protruding from it, sticking straight up. It looked like a challenge. So I approached it carefully and placed my right foot on top of the nail. My red Chuck Taylor sneakers—dirty from outdoor adventures—had never failed me before.

I slowly shifted my weight onto my right foot, balancing carefully. For a few seconds, I felt like Adonis—hands out, steady, entirely sure of myself. Then, in an instant, everything changed. With a heavy thud, my foot fell straight down onto the nail. It pierced through the sole of my shoe, through my foot, and stuck out the top—at least 11 inches of rusty gutter nail now impaling me to the debris below.

A jolt of pain shot through my leg. I gasped—a high-pitched, involuntary sound. The street around me blurred. I panicked. Did Mike or Mac see me? I looked around. No one had noticed. I tried to remain calm, but I was nailed to the ground—literally. I tried to pull away. The pain was excruciating. Tears welled up. My foot was anchored, and panic set in. I yanked once. Twice. On the third try, the nail tore through, leaving six inches still sticking out of my foot. I fell.

Mac saw me and shouted, "Bobby, you okay?" I replied, "No!"

Mac jumped from the roof, rushed over, and assessed the situation. Without warning, he grabbed my foot and yanked it off the nail. I stumbled up, screamed, and looked down— blood everywhere, my shoe destroyed. Mac told me to go home and get help. The walk home was brutal. My right foot curled, white sock blood-soaked, shoe in hand. I limped the entire way, trying not to cry. When I opened the front door, my father—reading the newspaper—looked up and went pale.

I showed him my foot. He dropped the paper and jumped up. My throat was tight with sobs. I couldn't speak. I just lifted my foot, bloodied and swollen. My dad was immediately concerned—and angry. He scooped me up, and despite his temper, his presence was a comfort. The trip to the doctor was a blur: antiseptic smells, bandages, and a painful tetanus shot. The wound was cleaned, but the trauma lingered.

The experience left a scar—physically and emotionally. It instilled a caution I hadn't had before and a respect for pain, risk, and the unexpected. I don't feel the pain any longer, but I do feel and remember the lessons learned.

Leadership in the Chaos

There's a leadership lesson buried in this story, just like there was a nail buried in my foot.

Sometimes, chaos shows up unannounced. One minute, you're balancing confidently; the next, you're impaled by something you didn't see coming. Leadership is about what happens next, how you respond when the pain hits, how you move when everything says stay still.

Think of Ernest Shackleton, the famed polar explorer and the epitome of leadership through chaos. In 1914, he led the Imperial Trans-Antarctic Expedition, an ambitious plan to traverse Antarctica. But soon after setting sail, disaster struck. His ship, the Endurance, became trapped in ice and was slowly crushed, leaving Shackleton and his crew stranded in one of the harshest environments on Earth.

They were isolated, freezing, with limited food, no communication, and no hope of immediate rescue. Shackleton could have folded. Instead, he doubled down on leadership. He kept morale high. He made hard calls. And when the situation grew desperate, he took matters into his own hands. Shackleton and five of his men set out in a small lifeboat across 800 miles of some of the roughest seas in the world, aiming for South Georgia Island. The journey was grueling—freezing temperatures, mountainous seas, relentless storms—but they made it. Once there, they had to cross uncharted, glacier-covered mountains just to reach a whaling station.

Most leaders would've stopped there. Not Shackleton. He immediately began organizing rescue missions for the 22 men left behind. After several failed attempts blocked by ice and weather, he finally succeeded. Every single man was saved. Not one life was lost.

Now, that is leadership. That's refusing to give up, even when all hope is gone. That's recognizing the nail in your foot and pushing through anyway. Leadership doesn't always look like triumph. Sometimes, it seems like limping home. It's like pulling your foot off the nail, like doing the thing that hurts so you can move forward. It's not about the wound. It's about the will.

Leaders don't avoid the nail. They learn from it. They don't just conquer chaos. They limp through it and lead anyway.

"You miss 100% of the shots

you don't take."

—Wayne Gretzky

6

YOU DON'T KNOW WHAT YOU DON'T KNOW

Let's face facts. The older I get, the more I realize how much I still have to learn. The more I understand about science, history, leadership, and motivation, the more I realize I don't know. And that's the point: you don't know what you don't know. This applies to almost everything in life. We know what we've been taught, what we've experienced, what we've seen firsthand. But beyond that? There's a vast ocean of information, perspectives, and truth that we've never even imagined.

At least I'm aware of that now. Many people aren't. We all know someone who thinks they know everything, who's never wrong—until they are. Let me explain. When

I attended school in the 1970s, I learned things about humans, evolution, history, and the solar system that I later discovered were utterly false. Not because my teachers were lying to me but because they were teaching what *they* had been taught. Since then, advances in science and discovery have proven much of it wrong. For example, I was taught Pluto was a planet. As of 2006? It's a dwarf planet. There aren't nine planets anymore. There are eight.

For example, I was never taught about one of the worst atrocities on American soil—the 1921 Tulsa Race Massacre in the Greenwood District. It was covered up and never mentioned in school. I didn't even hear about it until I was nearly 50. How is that possible? In the early 20th century, Greenwood was a thriving African American community, often referred to as "Black Wall Street." On May 31 and June 1, 1921, a white mob—some of them armed and deputized by local authorities—attacked the neighborhood. Over 35 square blocks were destroyed. Homes and businesses were burned to the ground. An estimated 300 people were killed, and thousands more were left homeless. It was the first time in U.S. history that American citizens were bombed from the air—by other Americans. And yet, for decades, this event was ignored or intentionally erased from textbooks and public discourse.

I was told giant squid were extinct. Then, in 2006, a 24-foot squid was found off the coast of Japan. As a kid, I watched *In Search Of* with Leonard Nimoy every week, hoping they'd find Bigfoot or the Loch Ness Monster. No giant squid back then. We were just wrong. And not just a one-time discovery— giant squid sightings and captures have since continued, providing direct proof of the existence of these elusive deep-sea creatures. The first images of a living giant squid in its natural habitat weren't even captured until 2004, and the first video wasn't recorded until 2012. For centuries, they were mythologized as sea monsters—like the Kraken—but now we know they're real. Mysterious, rare, but very real. This is just another example of how science evolves and how much we still don't know.

So, why are we humans so confident all the time? Why do we criticize, denounce, lecture, and judge when so much of what we think we "know" might be wrong? The human experience is defined less by what we know and more by what we don't. And yet, we continue to preach with confidence, often with no real knowledge.

"You don't know what you don't know" isn't just a clever phrase. It's a reality—especially in the unpredictable world we live in. This doesn't mean life is chaos. But it does mean we're operating on assumptions, guesses, and past experiences. And that blind spot affects everything: our decisions, our relationships, our leadership.

Think about it. We think we understand life, but we don't see the emotional currents coming, the chance encounters that change everything, or the quiet shifts inside ourselves that alter our direction. Life unfolds in ways we can't foresee. We try to plan. We study data. We hire consultants. But the world isn't a spreadsheet. One small, unforeseen event—a butterfly flapping its wings halfway around the globe—can cascade into something that changes our lives forever. We're all just sailing through uncertainty, guided only by what we know *so far*.

Love is the same. We think we know what it looks like, what it should feel like, where it should go. But love is unpredictable. We can't foresee its depth, or the pain, or the ways it will evolve. Love is an uncharted ocean. So is leadership.

Leadership in the face of the unknown requires humility, adaptability, and a willingness to learn and grow. It's not about controlling chaos. It's about thriving within it. Great leaders don't wait to have all the information. They act with what they have, stay flexible, and admit when they're wrong. They build cultures where learning is constant, where mistakes become fuel for growth.

This mindset isn't easy. It takes courage to lead in ambiguous situations. But this is where the best leaders are forged. Not in control, but in uncertainty. Not in knowing but in being open to the unknown. Acknowledging what we don't know makes us better leaders, better partners, better people. It keeps us curious. It keeps us humble. And it builds resilience—because we stop clinging to false certainty and start embracing discovery. We learn. We grow. We lead anyway.

Leadership Moment: Embracing Uncertainty

The phrase "you don't know what you don't know" is not an excuse to stop trying. It's an invitation to start learning. In leadership, assuming you know everything is a path to disaster. The best leaders are students first. They ask questions. They listen. They stay open.

Leadership isn't about having all the answers. It's about navigating through the fog, adjusting as you go, and helping others do the same. It's being honest when you hit unknown territory and courageous enough to take the next step anyway. That's what separates leaders from followers. In a world where change is constant, and certainty is a myth, this mindset isn't optional. It's essential.

Leaders who thrive in uncertainty aren't superhuman. They just understand a simple truth:

You don't know what you don't know. But you can learn. You can adapt. And you can lead anyway.

"The future belongs to those who believe in the beauty of their dreams."

—Eleanor Roosevelt

7

YOU'RE NOT ALWAYS THE PERSON YOU THOUGHT YOU WERE

The other day, I was talking to a colleague of mine about work. It was supposed to be a quick call—she was driving into the office, and I was heading into a meeting. Hands-free, in-transit, and routine. Something people do millions of times a day.

Then, mid-sentence, it happened. A sharp screech of tires. A scream. Then, a terrible series of crunches and crashes. Metal slamming metal. Again. Again. Again. I froze, the phone still to my ear, helpless. The chaos on the other end of the call unfolded in real time. And then—nothing. Just silence.

I called out her name. No answer. Just the distant sound of wind or static.

People at my meeting were watching me, waiting. I stepped back from the doorway and tried again: "Can you hear me? Are you okay?" Still no response. That meeting could wait.

Fact: Chaos doesn't make appointments. It doesn't give you a heads-up. It crashes in. And in that moment, everything I thought was urgent… wasn't. Eventually, she came back on the line—breathless, shaken. "There are cars everywhere. I'm in the middle of the Tollway."

Let me explain something about Dallas, Texas. The Tollway is not your average highway. It's more like a racetrack wrapped in concrete. There is no shoulder, no room for mistakes—just walls. And people doing 90 mph with a coffee in one hand and their phone in the other.

Now picture her—stopped sideways in rush hour, cars wrecked all around her. Nowhere to go. Nowhere to hide. I told her to stay in the car, seatbelt on unless she saw flames. We stayed on the phone until traffic stopped and sirens blared in the distance. I told her to call her husband. Then I told her to breathe. Meanwhile, the meeting I had prepared to attend for two weeks? Still going. I wasn't there. Chaos had rewritten my priorities.

That's what life does. It changes us. One moment, one phone call, one near tragedy— and suddenly, you're not the person you were ten minutes ago. The invincibility you carried fades. The urgency of your schedule dissolves. The person you *thought* you were gets stripped down. And a different version starts to emerge.

I come from a law enforcement and special operations background. I was trained to remain calm in chaotic situations. I prided myself on being a robotic, mission-focused individual. But age softens edges. Experience changes reflexes. Now, I weigh humanity alongside mission. Nothing lasts forever. Not your job. Not your body. Not even your identity. Who you are is constantly being rewritten by what you've lived through.

The fierce ambition of our youth dims under responsibility. The certainties of our twenties make way for the wisdom—and doubt—of our forties and fifties. We don't bounce back the same. And what we thought mattered most often fades. And yet… this is not failure. This is growth.

The roles we play—student, parent, partner, professional—each shape us. The transitions refine us. The crises awaken us. The joys surprise us. And the losses carve out space inside us for greater depth and empathy. To lead through this? To lead through chaos and transformation? You have to be willing to change. To let go of who you thought you were. To hold space for who you are becoming. That's not easy. But it's real.

And it's in these moments where you choose the call over the meeting, the human over the hustle, that your authentic leadership shows.

Leadership Moment: You Are Evolving

The leader you were yesterday isn't the one you need to be today. And the leader you are today? Not built to handle tomorrow, unless you grow. Leadership demands evolution. It's not about clinging to old successes or former mindsets. It's about adapting to the present and preparing for what's next.

Sometimes, life throws a wreck in your path to wake you up. To remind you what really matters. To call out the leader within you who's been buried under your to-do list. It takes courage to change. But the best leaders don't resist it. They let experience refine them. They let crisis reframe them. And they walk forward, not with all the answers, but with a willingness to keep becoming.

Because that's what leadership is. Not a title. Not a role. It's a constant act of becoming. And that version of you? The one shaped by empathy, chaos, and presence? That's the one people will follow.

"Anyone can hold the helm

when the sea is calm."

—Publilius Syrus

8

LEAD THROUGH
THE NOISE

It feels like navigating the complexities of today's society is more complicated than it was when I was young—by a lot. It's like walking through a minefield, where social chaos lurks at every turn, ready to explode. Issues are louder, stakes feel higher, and every word or opinion can become a lightning rod. It seems like you can't say or do anything without risking misinterpretation, offense, or backlash. The world feels louder, angrier, and more fragmented. Social media throws gasoline on every disagreement. News cycles are endless and overwhelming. Public discourse has turned into a minefield of trigger words and tribal loyalties. Even trying to stay neutral or quiet can make you a target. And for many people, it's exhausting.

And yet, despite all of it, building a positive life is still possible. It requires conscious effort, intentional choices, and a serious commitment to protecting your peace. For me, it starts with prioritizing inner calm, cultivating meaningful relationships, and focusing only on what I can control.

I'll talk about this a lot because, like you, I'm a work in progress. I let too many things get to me. I obsess over what I can't control. I overthink. I'm my own worst critic.

First, I've learned to limit my exposure to sensationalized news and toxic social media. I'm not perfect, far from it. I've spent too many nights scrolling headlines that only heightened my anxiety. I'm trying now to block out the noise. I mute negativity, avoid pointless arguments, and only follow content that inspires or educates me. If someone is consistently negative or inflammatory? Blocked. Life's too short.

Self-awareness is another anchor. Knowing my values and recognizing what triggers me has helped keep me grounded. I reflect often when I'm flying, mowing the lawn, or writing. That space for honest thought helps me recalibrate. It's part of how I reset.

Relationships are another critical buffer. I've learned to invest in the people who truly matter—friends and family who support, challenge, and care. Life is noisy, but real connection clears the static. I've found that meaningful conversation, shared time, and simple presence matter more than a thousand likes or retweets.

Purpose also matters. Whether it's volunteering, building something worthwhile, or helping someone in need, contributing gives me direction. It realigns me. It reminds me that I'm not powerless in the face of chaos.

Physical and mental health are foundational, too. I ride my bike. I walk. I try to sleep better and eat better. Not because it's easy because it keeps me functional. And when I can, I turn to nature, mindfulness, or writing to decompress. Everyone needs an off-ramp.

Gratitude helps, too. I try to stay focused on the good, however small. Sometimes, yes that means journaling. Sometimes, it's just pausing to notice what didn't go wrong. I'm learning that even in a chaotic world, peace is possible if I choose where to focus. I also try to adopt a growth mindset. Challenges are frustrating. But if I step back, most setbacks contain a lesson. Adaptability is a muscle. It strengthens with use.

Establishing boundaries has been huge. In today's hyper-connected world, you have to protect your time and energy like your life depends on it because, in a way, it does. Saying no is hard. But burnout is worse.

And it matters that we live ethically, too. I try to support businesses that align with my values. I try to be aware of what I consume and how it affects others. Little choices add up. Acts of kindness still matter. Maybe now more than ever. Even small gestures like a compliment, a helping hand, a text that says, "thinking of you" can ripple farther than we realize. We need more of that.

And we need to avoid toxicity. That includes people, places, and mindsets. I surround myself with people who challenge me to grow, but who also bring peace. That balance is critical.

Creativity helps, too. Writing, reading, reflecting. Any form of expression that makes me feel alive or understood. It's a release valve.

And at the end of the day? It's about self-care and self-compassion. None of us have it all figured out. But if we can be kind to ourselves and give ourselves grace. When we do, we'll have more to offer others. Resilience isn't perfection. It's the ability to keep showing up.

In the middle of all this social chaos, the key is hope. I hope that things can improve. I hope we can improve. I hope that the next moment might bring something meaningful.

Leadership Moment: Peace Is a Choice

In a world addicted to outrage, leaders who model calm become beacons. You don't have to mirror the chaos. You can rise above it. When you practice self-discipline in your emotions, focus on what truly matters, and prioritize meaningful connection over meaningless noise, you lead. Leadership doesn't always look like a rallying cry or a viral post. Sometimes, it's the quiet choice to breathe instead of react. To listen instead of shout. To build instead of tear down.

Calm is not weakness. It's control. It's power under restraint. It's the rare strength of someone who knows who they are and refuses to let the external world rewrite their internal script. In moments of pressure, panic, or polarization, calm leaders don't just steady themselves—they steady others. And make no mistake: people are watching. They're not drawn to the loudest person in the room; they're drawn to the one who keeps their composure when everyone else is unraveling. That kind of presence is rare and unforgettable.

"What you get by achieving your goals is not as important as what you become by achieving your goals."

—Zig Ziglar

9

LEAD WITH PURPOSE

I find that so many people today feel like they're drifting. They go through the motions—waking up, going to work, reacting to whatever life throws at them—but they don't feel like they're driving anything forward. They're not leading; they're being led by circumstance. Whether it's in business, family, or personal growth, the problem isn't lack of potential, it's lack of direction.

When you don't know where you're going or why you're going there, even the most substantial effort can lead to burnout or breakdown. This chapter about something most leaders overlook: the power of purposeful movement. It's not just about hustle. It's about intention, awareness, and the discipline to respond instead of react.

I learned this not in a boardroom or classroom but behind a horse, holding the reins. The smell of liniment and sweet feed was my baby powder. Instead of lullabies, I fell asleep to the rhythmic thud of hooves on the training track at our farm just outside Wilmington. My playground wasn't a swing set, but the dusty barn aisles and my best friends were the gentle giants with names like "John Hervey," "Race Worthy" and "Sneaky Chimes."

My father, a man whose hands were permanently calloused but whose touch with a horse was feather-light, lived and breathed harness racing. And from the moment I could walk, I was right there beside him. He never forced the world of horses on me, but the allure of the barn and the track was irresistible. My earliest memories are a blur of helping him muck stalls, filling water buckets that seemed twice my size, and carefully brushing the sleek coats of our horses. I'd perch on overturned buckets, watching him work, my small hands mimicking his movements as he meticulously cleaned tack or adjusted a harness. He was patient, always teaching by doing, and I absorbed every detail.

By the time I was ten, I was leading horses to and from the track, my petite frame dwarfed by their massive bodies. Dad would walk beside me, explaining their gaits, their temperaments, and the subtle cues that could only be learned through time and touch. He'd explain the intricacies of shoeing, the importance of a balanced diet, and the delicate art of reading a horse's mood.

The training track became my classroom. I'd sit beside Dad in the jog cart, the wind whipping through my hair as we circled the oval. He'd let me hold the reins for short stretches, my knuckles white with concentration as I tried to feel the rhythm of the horse beneath me. "Feel him, son," he'd say. "Listen to what he's telling you."

Weekends were spent at the local fairgrounds and racetracks, the air buzzing with energy. The vibrant silks of the drivers, the roar of the crowd, the pounding of hooves. It was a symphony of adrenaline. Dad would let me sit in the sulky after races, the worn leather and the scent of sweat and dirt becoming a part of who I was.

I didn't just love being around horses. I was consumed by it. I studied the great drivers, watched race tapes until they wore out, and practiced with our older horses. My passion became a purpose. I knew I wanted to drive. By sixteen, after years of matinee races and tireless preparation, I earned my provisional license. I had already raced at "Cowtown" Raceway in New Jersey and led in wins two years running. That small plastic card wasn't just a license—it was a key to my future.

Brandywine Raceway in Wilmington, Delaware, was the proving ground. It was a challenging circuit, home to legends and tough competitors. I started in overnight races, struggling at first. The competition was fierce, and every mistake was magnified. But I kept showing up, learning, and improving. My father was always close, reminding me to be patient as I learned about my horses, the track, and my competition.

Eventually, opportunity knocked. A stable with promising young horses took a chance on me. My dedication was paying off. With each win, my confidence grew. I began to read the races better, make sharper decisions, and drive with instinct. The Brandywine crowd, once intimidating, became familiar. Their cheers were fuel.

Then came the accident. I was piloting "Cicero Nugget," a fan favorite when he veered violently and launched himself over the guardrail. In a flash, I was thrown. Eight horses behind us had no chance to avoid the chaos. I remember hooves, metal, and then blackness. I woke up broken. Hospital beds replaced the barn. My body hurt. My spirit ached. I doubted everything. But I couldn't let it go. The fire wasn't out.

Recovery was long and painful. But the memory of what I loved pulled me forward. Eventually, I returned to the track. Tentative at first, then stronger with every race. One afternoon, behind a steady mare named "Marnies Hare," I surged past the leaders and crossed the finish line first. The crowd erupted. It was more than a win. It was a resurrection. A reminder that even when dreams shatter, they can be rebuilt.

Leadership Moment: Purpose in Motion

What does this have to do with leadership? Everything. Leadership is about understanding what moves people—and what stops them. Horses taught me that power without purpose is dangerous. They can bolt, veer, crash. But harnessed properly, with clear direction, their strength becomes unstoppable.

Leading others begins with learning to lead yourself, which means knowing your path, understanding your team, and adjusting to every shift in rhythm. It requires study, repetition, humility, and resilience. Sometimes, you'll crash. That's real. But if you get up, keep showing up, and move forward with intention, people will follow you. Not because you're perfect, but because you've proven you won't quit.

Move with a purpose. Because when you don't, chaos takes the reins. And when you do? That's when you lead anyway.

"You lose the respect of the

best when you don't deal

properly with the worst."

—John Maxwell

10

BOUNDARIES BITE

Leadership isn't just about vision and execution. It's about boundaries. Every team, no matter how high-performing, has unspoken lines that can get crossed if left unchecked. In today's culture of blurred work-life balance, some people forget where the job ends and where personal issues begin. When policies aren't clear, or leadership goes silent, confusion takes over, and sometimes, so does chaos. This story may seem bizarre on the surface, but it's a window into a larger problem: what happens when clarity is missing and no one knows where the boundaries are anymore?

When you're stepping into a new leadership role, the last thing you expect is to be growled at by a dog. But in today's work environments, where boundaries blur, expectations shift, and personal challenges spill into the professional space, strange things happen. And sometimes, those peculiar things reveal something far more important than the incident itself: they show you how people handle conflict, fear, and authority. This is one of those stories.

The dim hallway stretched before me, a stark contrast to the brightly lit offices I'd just left. As the new CEO, I was making my rounds, trying to get a feel for the company's atmosphere and rhythm. A soft glow emanated from one of the rooms, an anomaly in the otherwise uniformly lit floor. Curiosity piqued, I approached.

Pushing the door open, I was met with near darkness. The only light came from the computer screen, illuminating a lone figure hunched over the keyboard. It was a junior programmer, a woman I hadn't yet met. A sense of unease settled over me. Why were the lights off? Was she alright?

"Hello?" I called out, my voice a low rumble in the quiet room. She startled, her posture stiffening. As my eyes adjusted to the dimness, I noticed something large and dark beneath her desk—a dog. A rather large one, it seemed.

Intrigued, I crouched to get a better look. It was a beautiful animal, its fur a deep, glossy black. I reached out a hand to pet it, a natural gesture of friendliness.

"Don't," she said sharply, her voice tight. "He bites."

I froze. "He bites?"

"Yes," she confirmed, not turning away from her screen. "He's… protective."

"Protective of what?" I asked. "You? This desk?"

"He's mine. I brought him in," she said simply as if that explained everything.

"You brought a dog—that bites—to the office? Without asking?"

She shrugged. "If you don't touch him or come near me, he won't bite."

I stepped back, suddenly very aware of the low growl vibrating from beneath her desk.

"That's not the point," I said, working to keep my voice calm. "This is a workplace. We have a policy about animals. And about safety. You just told me this dog will bite."

"Only if he feels threatened," she insisted.

"I reached out to pet him," I replied. "That's not exactly threatening."

She said nothing.

"Look, I get it. Maybe you're going through something. Maybe you didn't have anyone to watch him. But this is a serious issue. If he bites someone—a client, another employee, me—we have a major liability."

"I didn't think it would be a problem," she mumbled.

"It is a problem," I said, more gently now. "You have to take him home. Now."

"But I have a deadline," she protested.

"We'll adjust. We'll work with you. But the dog can't stay."

She stared at the screen a moment longer, then slowly reached for the leash.

I stood by the door as she coaxed the dog out from under the desk. He gave me one last growl on the way out. I shut the door behind them.

That moment wasn't about a dog. It was about boundaries, expectations, and leadership under pressure. It was about how we handle the absurd, the emotional, the things that shouldn't happen but do.

Leadership Moment: Clear Boundaries, Firm Leadership

As leaders, we often deal with surprises. They come without warning, an unexpected resignation, a sudden crisis, a personal issue brought into the workplace. But what defines our leadership is not the absence of these disruptions. It's how we handle them. That day, I learned something I've carried with me ever since: empathy and decisiveness are not opposites. They're partners. One without the other creates imbalance. You can be compassionate. You can listen, understand, and offer support. But leadership also requires the courage to draw a line.

People will bring their dogs to work— literally or metaphorically. They'll carry their stress, their baggage, their insecurities, their unpredictable emotions. Some of it will sit quietly under the desk. Some of it will growl. Your job isn't just to manage timelines or hit quarterly goals. Your job is to manage clarity. To lead with conviction even when the situation is murky. To be the person who says what needs to be said, even when it's uncomfortable.

Boundaries matter. Safety matters. Respect matters. Even when it feels like the humane thing is to bend the rules. And yes, sometimes the dog bites. But lead anyway. Because the team is watching. The culture is listening. And in those moments, your leadership is not just tested—it's revealed.

"If you can dream it,

you can do it."

—Walt Disney

11

WE LIVE ON

In a world that often feels like it's coming apart at the seams, learning how to live well—truly live—is a radical act. We're constantly bombarded by noise, pressure, and the need to perform or produce. But leadership, especially personal leadership, starts from the inside out. This chapter is about reclaiming that space, about remembering that no matter what life throws at us, we still have the power to choose how we respond. It's about pushing back against the tide of cynicism and exhaustion and choosing, instead, to live with intention.

Maybe you've been there. Perhaps you're there now. Life has shaped you in ways that are both beautiful and brutal. The experiences that once felt like detours or disasters might just be the very things that qualify you to live with a greater purpose. This isn't about perfection

It's about progress. It's about embracing the full scope of your humanity: the strengths, the weaknesses, the fears, the fire.

And most importantly, it's about permitting yourself to begin again. You can still grow. You can still change. You can still choose to live, truly live, starting right now.

The inevitable ups and downs in our lives. I try not to let them define me. I will let them refine me. Pain, loss, unexpected change, and, yes, joy, too, all have a way of carving out deeper places in the soul. These deep places are not something to fear. They are where strength lives. The chaos that life sometimes throws my way will not overwhelm me. I will learn to navigate it, to find the calm within the storm. Chaos is often a catalyst for growth, a necessary disruption that forces individuals and organizations to adapt and innovate. I've started to accept that truth. I will approach challenges with a clear mind and a steady hand, seeking solutions rather than succumbing to despair. I wonder why I'm getting like this at my age instead of when I was younger. Never mind. Don't answer that. We all mature at different speeds.

Triumphs, when they arrive, will be celebrated with humility and gratitude. I will acknowledge the effort and perseverance that led to success, and I will share my joy with those who have supported me along the way. I understand that true triumph lies not only in achieving goals but in the character developed along the way. I will reflect on what made me succeed. Was it grit, faith, community, grace? All of it? Maybe. Probably. And that's worth honoring.

I will strive to be better, not for the sake of external validation but for the inherent satisfaction of personal growth. This matters to me. I will seek knowledge, cultivate wisdom, and refine my skills. I will challenge myself to step outside my comfort zone, to embrace new experiences, and to expand my horizons. I don't want to be a man who peaks early. I want to keep climbing. Even if the mountain looks different at 50 than it did at 30.

Leading myself with respect for myself and others is paramount. I will adhere to a strong moral compass, acting with integrity and authenticity. I will be accountable for my actions, taking responsibility for my mistakes and learning from them. Most people, including me, can be much better at this. I will strive to be a man of my word, trustworthy, dependable, humble. Even if I am already, I will try to be better. The moment we stop striving is the moment we start settling. I'm not ready to settle yet.

If the opportunity arises, I will lead others with the same honor and integrity. I will inspire and empower those around me, fostering a culture of respect, collaboration, and mutual support. I understand now that authentic leadership isn't about wielding power. It's about serving. It's about presence. It's about showing up again and again, even when you're tired or uncertain or heartbroken.

We should all try to cultivate a deep appreciation for the simple joys of life: a warm sunrise, a shared laugh, a moment of quiet contemplation or solitude. I like solitude. I like it a lot. In it, I find peace. I will appreciate beauty every day, recognizing the extraordinary in the ordinary. I will practice gratitude, acknowledging the abundance of blessings in my life. Gratitude isn't about being fake happy. It's about being present.

I will try harder to nurture my relationships, valuing the connections I too often take for granted. I'm not great at this. I'm working on it. I have family, friends, and loved ones. I will strive to be more present and engaged in my interactions, listening with empathy and speaking with kindness. I want to be a source of support and encouragement. Not just a doer. Not just a fixer. A presence.

I will prioritize my physical and mental well-being, recognizing that a healthy body and mind are essential for a fulfilling life. I will try to engage in regular exercise, nourish my body with wholesome food, and prioritize adequate rest. I will practice mindfulness, cultivating inner peace and resilience when I can. I've learned this the hard way: if you don't take care of yourself, everything else eventually falls apart. No matter how strong you think you are.

I want to pursue my passions with enthusiasm and dedication. I will seek out activities that bring me joy and fulfillment, and I will dedicate my time and energy to them. I will understand that passion is a driving force, fueling motivation and creativity. This may be writing. Or mentoring. Or something I haven't discovered yet. I'm still figuring it out. And that's ok!

I will embrace the challenges that come my way, viewing them as opportunities for growth and learning. I will not shy away from adversity but rather face it with courage and determination. Setbacks are not detours—they are part of the road. I will understand that they can ultimately lead to greater strength and resilience.

I want to cultivate a positive mindset, focusing on the reasonable and finding solutions to problems. I will avoid dwelling on negativity and instead seek out opportunities for growth and improvement. I will understand that my attitude shapes my reality. Not everything can be controlled, but a great deal can be influenced, starting with my perspective.

I will foster a lifelong learner's mindset. I will read widely, engage in meaningful conversations, and explore new ideas. I will understand that learning is a continuous process and that there is always more to discover. I will practice self-compassion, treating myself with the same kindness and understanding that I try to extend to others. I will forgive myself. We all need to do this more. I will move forward.

Cultivating a sense of purpose is important at any age, in any role. I will identify my values and align my actions with them. I will seek out opportunities to make a positive impact on the world, however small. A life of purpose is a life of meaning.

And I want to be a source of inspiration. Not because I've got all the answers but because I've wrestled with real questions. Because I've failed and gotten up. Because I've doubted and still believed. I will share my story—my resilience, my setbacks, my faith that we will all live on. And that life, as messy as it is, is still worth leaning into.

We live on. Through chaos. Through triumph. Through it all.

"That which does not kill us

makes us stronger."

—Friedrich Nietzsche

12

BEST MAN

The journey of life is often marked by unexpected twists and turns, encompassing both moments of joy and those of chaos and tragedy. Yet, within these myriads of experiences lies the potential for remarkable growth and success. As human beings, we possess an inherent resilience that enables us to navigate life's storms and emerge stronger, wiser, and more determined.

Whatever life throws our way, whether it be personal challenges, professional setbacks, or unforeseen circumstances, serves as a crucible for our character. It tests our limits, pushes us beyond our comfort zone, and forces us to adapt and evolve. We should embrace these challenges as opportunities for growth, recognizing that they are not meant to break us but to refine us. Positive mind set.

During the chaos, I find solace in my inner strength. I draw upon my resilience, my unwavering belief in myself, and my determination to overcome obstacles. I learn to navigate through the storm, to find calm amidst the chaos, and to emerge stronger than before. This takes practice.

As we navigate the complexities of our lives and work, we should strive to be guided by a vision of success that is not defined by external validation or material possessions. Most success lies in the ability to live authentically, pursue passions with unwavering dedication, and make a positive impact on the world around us.

With each triumph, we have likely led and motivated ourselves, as well as others, in the process. I am reminded of the inner strength and resilience we all possess, yet often don't realize it. As a human being, I possess extraordinary resilience and determination. We should try to embrace the chaos of life, not as an adversary but as an opportunity for growth and transformation. Not frustration or doubt.

Don't get me wrong, I still get upset at things some days. However, I will try to navigate through the storms, emerge stronger, and achieve success/triumphs on my terms. My journey is not about reaching a destination but about the continuous evolution of my character, the pursuit of my passions, and the positive impact I make on the world. This story is a perfect example of chaos, tragedy, survival, and leadership.

The Bell Boeing V-22 Osprey stands as a testament to ambitious engineering, a tiltrotor aircraft designed to bridge the gap between helicopter and fixed-wing capabilities. However, its development and operational history have been marred by a series of accidents, raising persistent concerns about its safety.

Developed by Bell Helicopter and Boeing Helicopters, the V-22 was envisioned to provide unparalleled operational flexibility. Its ability to take off and land vertically like a helicopter and then transition to horizontal flight for high-speed, long-range missions made it a highly desirable asset for the U.S. military.

However, the complexities of the tiltrotor design have contributed to a troubling accident record. As of November 2023, 16 V-22 Ospreys have been lost in crashes, resulting in the deaths of 62 people. Notably, four of these crashes occurred during the aircraft's developmental phase, from 1991 to 2000, claiming 30 lives. Since its operational debut in 2007, 12 more crashes and numerous incidents have resulted in 32 additional fatalities.

A History of Accidents and The Two That Affected Me

June 1991: A misfired flight control system caused a V-22 to strike the ground during a hover at New Castle County Airport, Delaware. The resulting impact and fire caused minor injuries. This incident highlighted the complexity of the V-22's control systems and the potential for errors to occur.

July 1992: A catastrophic engine failure led to a V-22 crashing into the Potomac River near Marine Corps Base Quantico. All seven individuals aboard perished. This accident, which was witnessed by the Department of Defense and industry officials, resulted in an 11-month grounding of the V-22 fleet.

Witness to Disaster: A First-Hand Account of the V-22 Osprey Crash at Wilmington Airport

In the 1980s and 1990s, I was a Delaware State Trooper. On this particular day, I was assigned to the north helicopter call sign "Trooper 4" as a Trooper Paramedic. It was summertime. Rich, the Trooper-Pilot, and I had just landed at the Delaware State Police helicopter hangar, which sat about 200 feet from the Boeing hangars at Wilmington Airport.

As we shut down the rotor blades, the familiar hum of the airport was shattered by a thunderous sound. A V-22 Osprey, visibly in distress, plummeted from the sky and crashed onto the tarmac. The sight was jarring: metal twisted, smoke rising, flames crackling. My body moved before my brain could process it.

Training kicked in. We immediately took off again, circling to assess the scene from above.

I radioed the fire board and called for rescue equipment and emergency crews. We landed closer to the wreckage, the heat from the fire already radiating outward. I jumped out, scanning for movement. In a YouTube video, if you ever see a guy in a blue flight suit and white helmet moving toward the blaze. That's me!

The V-22 was upside down, burning. There was chaos, but controlled chaos. First responders rushed, everyone, doing what they could. It was a moment I will never forget—the sheer helplessness of watching a technological marvel become a metal tomb and hoping, praying, for survivors.

A Friend's Fear: The V-22 Crash and a Pilot's Deep Concern

What haunted me most wasn't just the crash itself. It was the chilling fear that my best friend—Bob, my flight instructor, my

mentor, and the best man at my wedding—
might have been on board. Bob was a test
engineer for Boeing at the time and had
spoken to me many times about his fascina-
tion with the V-22. He knew its risks and its
promise. He had even been asked to consult
on the project.

When I saw the aircraft crash, my heart
dropped. I couldn't breathe. My mind raced:
Was he on that flight? Was he okay? I was able
to speak with the surviving crew—shaken but
alive. And I learned, with immense relief, that
Bob had not been on board.

But that relief was short-lived.

On July 20, 1992, I got the call while
I was at one of the Delaware beaches. A
pre-production V-22 Osprey had crashed
into the Potomac River near Quantico. All
seven people on board had died. Bob was one
of them.

I was the executor of his estate. The next
several years were filled with grief, paperwork, frustration, and unshakable sorrow.
Bob wasn't just a pilot or an engineer. He

was my friend, a man who loved the sky, who loved teaching others to fly, and who believed in pushing boundaries.

I can not count the many hours that Bob and I have spent in different airplanes together before his death. The picture on the front of the book is me flying a 1941 T-6 warbird over Texas. Something I never would have been able to do without Bob's leadership to me! The picture is a "thank you" to my friend

His loss, like that of so many others, is a poignant reminder that leadership is not just about strategy and vision. It's about courage. It's about risk. It's about showing up in hard places and doing the work, even when it costs you.

Bob did that. And I try every day to do the same.

"The art of life lies in a constant readjustment to our surroundings."

—Kakuzo Okakura

"Don't watch the clock; do

what it does. Keep going."

—Sam Levenson

CONCLUSION

LEAD ANYWAY

The title of this book was never meant to be a slogan. It was a survival strategy. A call to courage. A reminder that life will rarely hand you the perfect circumstances, the ideal team, or the pristine runway to lead the way you envisioned. Instead, life gives you turbulence. It gives you setbacks, late-night calls, unexpected diagnoses, personal betrayals, and public storms. And through all of it, you get to decide: lead anyway.

You've read my stories. Stories of struggle and strength. Of being knocked down and getting back up. Of flying through literal storms and navigating metaphorical ones. I've tried to be honest with you, because that's what leadership demands today. Not perfection, but presence. Not charisma, but character.

What you've hopefully discovered through these pages is that leadership isn't reserved for CEOs, special forces veterans, or first responders. Leadership is available to anyone willing to take responsibility for their response to chaos. It's a daily decision to act with courage, with clarity, and with conviction—even when no one is watching.

You've also seen how chaos comes in many forms: a broken economy, a betrayed friendship, a health scare, or a quiet, persistent voice telling you that you're not enough. Sometimes it arrives as a helicopter falling from the sky. Sometimes, it sneaks in as self-doubt or burnout. But it always invites the same response: rise. Stand up. Lead anyway.

And let me be clear—leading anyway doesn't mean ignoring your pain. It means honoring it. Learning from it. Channeling it. Leading anyway is about bringing your full self to the challenge, not pretending the challenge doesn't hurt. It's about staying soft-hearted while developing a thick skin. It's about listening deeply, even as you make tough decisions. And it's about building resilience—not through bravado, but through vulnerability and discipline.

I've sat across from world leaders and wounded friends. I've led elite teams and lost sleep over simple, human concerns. And I've learned this: the people who make the greatest impact in the world are the ones who choose to show up—again and again—despite the fear, despite the fatigue, despite the failures.

So here, at the end, I want to offer a few truths. Simple ones. Earned through hard seasons:

- You don't have to feel ready to take the first step.

- You don't have to have all the answers to make a difference.

- You don't have to wait until the storm passes to start leading.

You just have to show up.

I've said throughout this book that leadership is a human endeavor. It's not about hierarchy; it's about responsibility. It's not about the loudest voice; it's about the clearest one.

And in a world addicted to noise and outrage, what we need more than ever is leaders who are grounded, steady, and real. Leaders who lead anyway.

If you take anything from this book, let it be this: your story matters. Your chaos isn't a disqualifier. It's your curriculum. Your wounds don't discredit your leadership— they deepen it. Your setbacks aren't signs of weakness. They are proof that you've been in the fight.

And if you're still here—still learning, still struggling, still showing up—then you're already leading.

Leadership doesn't always come with applause. Often, it comes in quiet moments when you choose integrity over ease, service over ego, or discipline over drama. And the impact you make in those moments ripples far beyond what you may ever see.

Let me leave you with this: leadership is not a one-time decision. It is a lifestyle. It's not something you do. It's someone you become. And becoming takes time. Becoming takes hardship. Becoming is a journey full of false starts, awkward pivots, messy truths, and moments that humble you. But through it all, you learn to lead not in spite of the chaos—but because of it.

When I look back at my own leadership path—from the streets of Wilmington to the highest levels of national security—I don't remember every accolade. I remember the conversations that mattered. I remember the moments I didn't quit. I remember the people who needed someone to show up—and I chose to.

You're not leading just for today. You're building trust that lasts tomorrow. You're modeling steadiness for the next generation. You're writing a story that others will read and say, "Because they showed up, I did too."

So wherever you are today—whether you're at the start of your leadership journey or worn out from years on the front lines— know this: your presence still matters. Your influence still matters. Your story is still being written. And it's more powerful than you think.

Keep pressing forward. Keep choosing courage over comfort. Keep building, even when it feels like it's all falling apart. Keep believing that your best leadership moments might still be ahead of you.

Because the world doesn't need perfect leaders. It needs courageous ones.

And you, my friend, are more ready than you think.

Lead anyway.